Printed in the United States of America

ISBN TXU 697-523

15   14   13   12   11   10   21   20   19   18

Written and Published by
Carol and Francis Murphy
of Murphy Books

Chinco263@cf.com
Price: $20.00

Special Thanks to my wife, Carol, for all the years of support and love and specially for all of your help with my book.

DEDICATION

Dedicated to the 250 crewmen and officers of the USS Chincoteague and especially to those who lost their lives.

B-29 DOWN!

Choppy, white-capped seas stirred by buffeting winds splashed a heavy salty spray over the bow of the *"Chinc"* as it steamed northwest from the Solomon Islands in the South Pacific. The USS *Chincoteague* (AVP-24) was a destroyer-sized seaplane tender the length of a football field but much broader abeam than a destroyer. AVPs functioned as hotels, restaurants, gas stations, garages, medical clinics and movie theaters for assigned seaplane squadrons.

The *Chinc,* operating independently in the Southwest Pacific in 1944, received orders to proceed to Peleliu Island in the Palau Islands group to assume air-sea rescue duties. The Palaus are approximately 500 miles east of Mindanao Island in the Philippines and 1,000 miles west of the neutralized Japanese bastion at Truk.

AVPs, the "mother hens" to seaplane squadrons, performed yeoman service in patrolling war zones. The stubby little ships also tended PT-boat squadrons. The AVP's broad beam gave the ship extra space to accommodate squadron crews for extended periods of operation. It also had enough space astern to lift a plane aboard for repair and maintenance.

Upon arrival, we found Peleliu still occupied by remnants of the Japanese army. The 1st Marine Division under famed Lewis B. (Chesty) Puller, then a lieutenant colonel, had invaded Peleliu to capture the airfield on its southern tip. It was the largest Japanese air base in the Palaus and was needed to establish a bomber base for the U.S. Army Air Forces' use in the Philippine campaign.

The Army's 81st Infantry Regiment had attacked Angaur Island 10 miles south of Peleliu, without much resistance. It later rendered assistance to the Peleliu battle by first sending in its 321st and 323rd combat teams. The resistance on Peleliu was much greater than expected; the battle wore on to become one of the bloodiest island-hopping campaigns in the Pacific.

We dropped anchor near the base in a coral-protected bay called Kossel Roads, which was used as a small fleet anchorage. B-29 bombers were making daily sorties on the Philippines in preparation for the invasion and Gen. Douglas MacArthur's triumphant return.

Mid-morning, three days after our arrival, a message came in announcing that a U.S. bomber had gone down upon its return to the Peleliu base. Immediately we upped anchor, moved slowly out of the bay, picked up speed and began the search.

We patrolled all day without success, continuing the search after sunset. We steamed to the other side of the island to take advantage of a full moon. Japanese searchlights pierced the darkness and beamed back and forth, but they did not sweep low enough to spot the ship. Luck did not come our way that night, and we returned to Kossel Roads.

At dawn the next day, we continued the search with the help of a small Piper-sized Army aircraft. It is extremely difficult to spot an object in the chöppy waters of a vast ocean from the bridge of a ship. Nevertheless, at about noon the ship's pilot spotted a man hugging a deflated yellow life raft kept buoyant by what we later learned was a well-packed radio.

We sped to the location, then moved slowly to within 30 yards of the raft. Over the side went a cargo net. Into the water dove the chief boatswain's mate. At the same time, sailors manning the ship's bow fired rifles to ward off the sharks circling the life raft.

The boatswain's mate's only thought as he dove into the ocean was of a quick rescue. He was oblivious to the shark-infested waters and moved with the speed of an Olympic swimmer. He grabbed the man and hauled him into the cargo net. Both were pulled aboard by the anxious crew. The moment the man was safe on deck, in the arms of his savior, he collapsed into unconsciousness.

He was beyond the limits of exhaustion. The airman had clung to life with indomitable determination and unbelievable fortitude. Certainly, his persistence was proof of the axiom that a man's fight for survival brings forth unbelievable strengths.

After hours of deep sleep, the rescued airman woke up and took a long, hot shower. This alone was a luxury worth living for. Living on Peleliu on war rations in meager facilities offered no such pleasure. The refreshed airman donned clean clothes and followed the other men to the mess hall. There he encountered another indulgence – a hot meal topped off with a piece of pie à la mode.

The man's first words after he had thanked his rescuers and finished his repast were, "Where do I go to sign up for this man's Navy?" Undoubtedly, this fortunate airman returned home after the war with a different outlook on life.

This story of a downed B-29 airman is only one among many tales of the fight for survival during World War II. What greater satisfaction can there be than saving the life of a fellow warrior in the far reaches of a vast ocean in a time of worldwide turmoil?

INTRODUCTION

For the past year I have been thinking a lot about the USS Chincoteague, the bombing raids in the South Pacific. I have been trying to locate shipmates.

I began doing this as a result of ordering a picture of the Chincoteague with a list of four or five names of others who had ordered the picture. This started me on a nostalgic journey of my life in the Navy, my experiences on the Chincoteague and my life before this. I have felt I must put this on paper. Perhaps my grandchildren will be interested in reading this some day.

CHAPTER ONE

NORTH DAKOTA

To begin my story, I must start at the place of my birth. I was born at Sarles, North Dakota. It's a small town just south of the Canadian border. It also happened to be at the end of the Great Northern Branch Line from Lakota. My father was the conductor on that train. He met and married my mother, Nellie Gillin. She was the daughter of the local barber. I was the middle child in a family of eleven, seven girls and four boys.

We lived in a small two story house. I don't really remember how we all fit in this small house. I guess it had a lot to do with why I left home at such an early age.

We had no indoor plumbing. I don't think very many people did at that time. Everyone had an outhouse which was fine in the summer but kind of cold in the winter when it was 20 to 30 degrees below zero for days at a time. When we got up in the morning we would make a dash for the school house which was close. There were indoor restrooms there.

We had a furnace in the basement with a floor register. One of us, it seemed like I did it a lot, would fill it with coal at night, but by morning the fire was out and the house was freezing. There would be ice in the bucket with the drinking water.

Winter days were sometimes very cold. Most people raised in North Dakota can remember at least one day that was 50 degrees below zero.

Weather has moderated a lot in recent years, but there are still days of 20 degrees below zero.

Francis D. Murphy, Boot Camp, 1942

Sometimes there were blizzards that lasted all day or maybe up to three days. It had to be pretty bad before school closed.

Those were days to spend inside, if you didn't have to get out to go to a job. We listened to the radio, read books, playing cards and the women caught up on baking and sewing. Somebody would make fudge and pop popcorn.

I remember one beautiful March day in 1941. The sun was shining, water was running down the street from the melting snow. It was a Saturday, so the farmers were in town to do their shopping. A lot of the men were spending a time in the local tavern catching up on the gossip. A blizzard came up very suddenly and the temperature plummeted. There weren't storm warning like now, with all the modern technology.

Visibility was cut to zero and people were caught out on the highways or maybe even between the house and the barn. Many people perished during this storm.

I was going to go to my friend, Jim Stapleton's, house to play poker, but I didn't get very far. I walked right into a car I couldn't see and decided I better get back home if I could find the way. It was too tough out there for me.

My best friend was Billy Botsford. We were close to the same age and in the same grade in school. I guess we both liked to get into mischief too.

CHAPTER TWO

SKUNK HUNTING

It wasn't always mischief, because we liked to find a way to earn a little money too. A good way to do this was to hunt skunks. A skunk pelt was worth $1.50, a lot of money to us.

One time a skunk went into a culvert. I told Billy to crawl in and chase him out and I would wait on the other side and shoot him when he came out.

Well, you know what happened to Billy. Neither one of us smelled too good when we got to town. I don't remember how long it took for that to wear off, but it must have been several days. We went to the drugstore for something, but they told us we couldn't come in smelling like that.

Another time I borrowed a paring knife from a neighbor. She didn't ask what I was going to do with it, and was pretty upset when she found out. I wonder if she used the knife again? I doubt if it really hurt it after the smell wore off.

CHAPTER THREE

FARMS

From the time I was seven years old I would go out to farms to do whatever work I could. I guess I liked being on a farm, and away from all the kids at home.

I didn't like to be at home when my Dad was home either. He was away working on the railroad most of the time, but we didn't get along when he was there. Maybe we were too much alike - two stubborn Irishmen. He believed in the old adage spare the rod and spoil the child. Maybe it worked the wrong way with me. It filled me with bitterness and resentment that has been hard to get rid of.

My dad died in 1948, at the age of 70. I was in China and could not get back in time for the funeral.

One of the farms I like to go to was the John Ball Farm. Their youngest son, Everett, was a few years older than I was, but he tolerated me. They had a Shetland Pony named Sparkle. I liked to ride it and heard cattle. I helped Everett milk the cows too. He says I didn't milk very many, but I thought I did.

The Ball family sold their farm in 1935 and moved to Longview, Washington. I hated to have them leave. Their place was my second home. I guess they would have liked to take me along, but I'm sure Ma wouldn't have allowed that.

Everett and his wife, Claudia, still live at Kelso, Washington and we see each other often. Everett is still one of my best friends.

When I was 11 years old, I worked for Neil Nicholson. We were working with two binders. If anyone doesn't know what a binder is, it cuts the wheat or other grain and ties it into bundles. I had the lead one, pulled by four horses. We came to a swampy spot in the field and I used the whip on the horses' rumps and they trotted right through. Neil came behind and he got stuck. He sure wondered how I made it and he didn't.

After I got paid, Neil was going to New Rockford, a larger town. I went with him and bought new clothes for school. In New Rockford, I saw a city policeman in uniform. That was the first time I had ever seen one. When I was at Nicholson's, I would take a horse and buggy and go to Calvin, another small town that was near, to get the mail. He wasn't on the mail route and had a post office box.

The horse was named Fanny Air. She was retired from horse racing and was trained to trot. She was really rough to ride unless you could get her to gallop.

CHAPTER FOUR

SHOE SHINE MURPHY

My granddad, Daniel Gillin, was the town barber. He had two chairs, and also a room with a bathtub. Haircuts were $0.50, shaves were $0.25 and baths, $0.50. The baths were pretty popular with the farm hands, especially on Saturday night. The barber shop is still there, and the signs in the window says Gillin's Barber Shop and farther down, Baths. It is vacant and sad.

Granddad had a shoe shine box. I would go in there to shine shoes. When I wore one out, I built another one. I hitchhiked to dances to shine shoes. In fact, I hitchhiked to Montana, shining shoes. It was a good way to earn enough for food and a bed.

My uncle, Frank Gillin, was a barber, too. He kept the shop running until he died. I used to always go there for a haircut when I was in Sarles.

When I was a kid, Uncle Frank played ball with me. We would go bird hunting together. We had a dog named Chuck. He like to hunt too. We hunted for grouse and prairie chickens. He went to the barber shop during hunting season and stayed until it was over. Then he came home.

I hitchhiked to all the small towns to shine shoes at dances. There used to be a lot of dances. Probably every Saturday night there was one not too far away. A lot of the bands became famous later. I remember Lawrence Welk being at one of them.

County fairs at Langdon, North Dakota, and Rollette, North Dakota, gave more opportunities for earning money with my shoe shine box. Also rodeos at Dunseith, North Dakota.

It was at one of these rodeos at Dunseith that I decided to go to Great Falls, Montana, instead of going home.

Wayne's Inn was a popular road house just out of Rolla, North Dakota. Bill and Lena Wayne were friends of mine, so this is another good place to go. Sunday they
had roller skating.

One of the big events of the area was the Scottish Days at Calvin. This was mainly a Scottish settlement. There was a bagpipe band, with the Scotsmen wearing their kilts. There was a parade, band music, and all the people from far and near came for the event. It was a great opportunity for me and my shoe shine box. Of course, there was a dance in the evening. My nickname was "Shoe Shine Murphy".

CHAPTER FIVE

LEFT HOME

As I said, I decided to go to Great Falls. My sister, Bernice, lived there. She was married to Steve Enott.

I guess I got to Minot the first day and stayed overnight there, always shining shoes for expense money. At this time I was only 14. I don't know what I would have done if my son had pulled these stunts. Of course we only had one, so had more time to worry about him.

Then I went to Glasgow, Montana and shined shoes there, in front of Stan's Bar. They were building Fort Peck Dam at that time, so there were lot's of working men around.

When I got to Great Falls, of course I shined shoes. I worked on 1st Ave. South, in front of Helen Enott's bar. She was Steve's, and my other brother-in-law, Mike's sister. She was always good to me.

I was there about a month. Then I went back home and back to school.

CHAPTER SIX

QUIT SCHOOL

Billy Botsford and I got mad at one of the teachers, and we walked out of school the same day. That was the end of my formal education. I guess I really didn't see any reason why I should know any of this stuff.

It was the middle of February and 13 degrees below zero. My mother tried to talk me out of going, but I didn't listen to her. I probably didn't want to confront my dad.

When I got to be 16 years old, I worked as a Bell Hop at the Park Hotel. Eleven years later, my wife and I spent part of our honeymoon there.

Later I went to Seattle, because my oldest sister, Dorothy lived there. I worked for a time at the Bremerton Navy Yard.

I soon went back to Great Falls, and bell hopping at the Park, until I joined the Navy on October 10, 1942.

February, 1944.

CHAPTER SEVEN

IN THE NAVY

During the summer of 1942, after I was 18 years old, I started thinking about enlisting in the Military.

At first I thought the Marines was the place to be. They were a tough group, and I thought I was pretty tough. The physical for the Marines is tougher than the other branches of the service, and they turned me down because of a heart mummer.

I decided to try the Navy. They discovered the heart mummer also, but didn't think if was serious enough to keep me from doing what was required of me.

I have always been glad I joined the Navy. I had a good clean home. I always heard the Navy was a clean place, but they forgot to say who kept it clean. We soon found that out.

I enlisted at Great Falls and we were sent to Helena to be sworn in. From Helena and we were put on a train and sent to Farragut, Idaho.

A lot of you guys reading this, know about Farragut. The country was beautiful, with mountains all around and lakes near by. But the Indians wouldn't live there because of what they called "Cat Fever".

We arrived in the afternoon and were assigned to our barracks. We were assigned to Camp Binyon, Company 34/42. Camp Binyon was the first of many camps at Farragut, Idaho.

CHAPTER EIGHT

BOOT CAMP

We got up at 4:30 am the next day. After going to the Mess Hall for breakfast, we were sent to get our shots.

We stood in a line a mile long, at least it seemed like it. There was a corpsman standing on each side, armed with a needle, and you got it from both sides. Guys were dropping right and left. Some of them were so afraid to get a shot. It didn't bother me, I had had shots before.

Next we went to get our uniforms and other clothing. We were given boxes to put our civilian clothes in to be sent home. I bet Ma hated to get that box. She didn't really want me in the military. It must be almost like receiving the final remains.

Putting Navy Jumpers on with those sore arms was really a tough job. My arms hurt so bad I didn't think they would ever get better. Of course they did, and we went on with our training.

We went to classes to learn how to swim and to dive. I knew how to swim, but diving was new. We were required to jump off a 30 foot diving board. After we passed our swimming requirements, we went on to other instruction.

Every morning we went to the "Grinder" to march for a couple of hours. Then it snowed and we were marching in snow banks up to our butts. That wasn't easy.

After calisthenics we had breakfast, and back to the barracks to clean. Then we were marching again and it was time for a noon meal.

There was always something for us to do. Clean the barracks, march, calisthenics,
swimming.

Three times we went out on the Commando Course. I guess I didn't have too much trouble with that since I was small and wiry.

I got all my teeth fixed when I was at Farragut. I still have some of those fillings, 52
years later.

When Boot Camp was finished, we were given a ten day liberty. I took the train to Great Falls to see my sisters and their families.

CHAPTER NINE

BACK TO FARRAGUT

We wondered where we were going to go next. We thought of all kinds of exotic places. Maybe permanent duty in California, or how about Hawaii. Maybe Alaska. I sure didn't want that. I'd seen enough snow and below zero weather.

They loaded us on a troupe train and we pulled out at midnight. The train was running in BLACK OUT conditions. All the shades were drawn, so there would be no light leaking to the outside. We were always on the alert for enemy planes that might come over and drop bombs. We weren't that far from the coast.

In the morning we were at King Street Station in Seattle, Washington. They marched us from the train to the depot. From there down the street to the Ferry Landing.

We loaded on the Ferry and went across Puget Sound to Bremerton, Washington where there was a Navy Base.

We got additional training during the six weeks we were there. I guess we were actually waiting for our ship to be completed, but nobody told us anything. Of course during WWII everything was top secret.

CHAPTER TEN

KIRKLAND

Eventually we were transferred to Kirkland, Washington and assigned to our barracks there. When we went to Kirkland in l965, the barracks was still there. I took a picture of it. I was being used as a Civic Center. Some years later it burned.

During the time we were at Kirkland, we were sent to Pacific Beach to Gunnery School. Pacific Beach is near Aberdeen, Washington. We have gone up there to find this place. The Navy facility is still there. There didn't seem to be too much going on.

We went back to Kirkland and trained on 5" 38's'. We practiced loading a Dummy gun. The 5" 38 was a gun that was good for either aircraft or surface fighting. You could swing it all the way around, you could shoot straight out or into the air. We had four of them on our ship. I was assigned to the third one. We got plenty of training on those guns.

Barracks at Kirkland, Wa., April, 1965. These barracks burned to the ground in the 1970's.

CHAPTER ELEVEN

THE CHINCOTEAGUE

We received our orders! We were shipping out. We packed our gear and marched down to the docks of the Lake Washington Shipyards and boarded our ship. She was the USS Chincoteague AVP 24, a Sea Plane Tender which had just been completed and was ready for test runs and it's part in winning World War II.

The Chincoteague was built at Lake Washington Shipyards, Houghton, Washington. Houghton was right next door to Kirkland. It was the second Sea Plane Tender to be built by LWS. My sister Joey was a Welder's Helper and I tell her that's why it was such a tough ship. My brother-in-law, Bill Chitwood, also worked on it.

She was launched April 15, 1942, by Mrs.

The USS Chincoteague "on the ways", 1942.

Gordon Rowe. Mrs. Rowe said she grabbed the bottle like a baseball bat and hit hard. Champagne flew all over and shorted out the flash mechanism in a press photographer's camera.

The launching was a simple ceremony as this was war time. The public wasn't invited, but the hill in back of the shipyards was crowded with people watching.

The USS Chincoteague (pronounced shin-ca-teague) is named after an inlet on the east coast of Virginia. There is also a small island named Chincoteague, which has hundreds of wild horses which swam to the island after a Spanish Galleon shipwreck off shore in the 1600's. The ponies were being shipped to the Viceroy of Peru who prized them.

They were able to swim to shore and flourished there. Every year they have a round up and some of the ponies are sold.

Chincoteague is an Indian name meaning "swift flowing stream". To the Navy, the USS Chincoteague was officially known as the AVP 24.

The Chincoteague was not a large ship. It was

Commander Hobbs, the first Caption of the USS Chincoteague.

41.1 feet wide and a little longer than a football field. It was just a little larger than a destroyer.

It's purpose was to provide a floating base from which seaplanes could be refueled, replenish ammunition and be repaired. Also the seaplane crews came on board to rest when not on duty. I guess we were also a floating hotel and restaurant. Tenders were used for advance bases, going wherever they were needed. They were Mother Hen's to a brood of patrol planes.

CHAPTER TWELVE

ON OUR WAY

In a couple of hours we were under way. We left Kirkland and out of Lake Washington by way of the Ballard Locks into Puget Sound.

Our first destination was Bremerton where the Chincoteague was commissioned. Our Commander was Ira E. Hobbs, with a crew of 250 officers and sailors. One third of the men were experienced, two thirds were not.

The ship was commissioned April 12, 1943, one year after launching, and reported to the Pacific Fleet.

We left Bremerton and sailed to Bangor, Washington to load ammunition, bombs and torpedoes. We then went to Seattle, Washington, on April 25th, to load 100 octane gasoline for the airplanes, 85,000 gallons. While still in Seattle, we took on food stores. We were loaded with 260 pounds of celery, 1170 pounds of grapefruit, 75 pounds of lemons, 780 pounds of lettuce, 500 pounds of onions and 990 pounds of tomatoes from Pacific Fruit and Produce Co. That should have made a BIG salad. At Washington Co-op Egg and Poultry Co, in Seattle, Washington, we got 40 cases of eggs.

On May 1, the radio equipment was inspected by John F. Park, of Navy Yard Radio Lab. May 4th received on board 40 cases of potatoes, 2 cases of Vaccine for the Medical Department, 150 filled oxygen flasks and 1560 gallons of diesel fuel.

Wednesday, May 5th, the ships logs reported "stop taking on stores. Watertight doors were reported closed. At 8:00 p.m., reported Steaming as before; circled A-123 for inspection; resumed standard speed on base course 180T." We had completed a couple of weeks of Shake Down Cruises in the Puget Sound, and now we were under way.

CHAPTER THIRTEEN

THE PACIFIC OCEAN

The water off the coast of Washington and Oregon was so rough that everybody, including the Captain, got sick. I lasted until about 5 o'clock in the afternoon, everybody was throwing up and it finally got the best of me. I still get seasick when I go deep sea fishing, which my son has always thought was really funny.

The good thing about it was that it wasn't long before we went to bed for the night. After getting up at 5 in the morning, we went to bed about 8 or 9 o'clock.

At 5 am they came with a dish pan and hammer and woke us up. We would go on about our duty of sweeping and swabbing. I mentioned before that the Navy is a very clean place, and we were sure busy keeping it that way. We had cleaning and painting jobs all day.

We didn't do any gunnery practice on the way down there, but the rough water was sure hard on the guys. We pulled into San Francisco for four hours. The Skipper's wife lived there. No one else was allowed to leave the ship.

CHAPTER FOURTEEN

SAN DIEGO

We went back out to sea and on down to San Diego. While we were there we did more Shake Down Cruises, testing depth charges and testing the engines. Also, we fired the guns to see where the shells would end up.

We shot at drones and at targets out in the ocean. Drones were remote control planes used for target practice. We'd go out in the morning and back in at night. We did this for about two weeks.

An emergency appendectomy was preformed by the ship doctor during the time we were on our way from Puget Sound to San Diego. The Seaman was transferred to the Navy Hospital at San Diego.

Work wasn't the only thing the crew of the USS Chincoteague did while in San Diego as seen here relaxing at a pub before shipping out. 1943

CHAPTER FIFTEEN

SAILING THE BLUE OCEAN

After taking on supplies, fuel, and our numerous shake down cruises and practice shooting, we were on our way.

By June 20, 1943, we were in Pearl Harbor. Nothing out of the ordinary occurred while we made this crossing.

At Pearl Harbor we took on 300 pounds of fresh white bread. This was a treat for everyone.

June 21st, twenty-one officers and seventy-nine enlisted men from a Marine Detachment came on board for transportation. Also, one officer and fifty-four enlisted men from a Marine Flight Air Wing. We were given a short liberty while at Pearl Harbor.

I told my wife for years that I had been to Hawaii and there wasn't anything there. There wasn't anything to see. I never really convinced her and she finally talked me into going. We went 10 more times after that, and made a lot of friends.

After refueling and taking on board 300 pounds of fresh pineapple and 200 pounds of tomatoes, we were once more under way.

We took the Marines to the Ellis Islands and to Espiritu Santo in the New Hebrides Islands.

Recently one of the Marines called me and asked if I remembered taking a bunch of them to the Islands. After telling him I did, he said he was the only one left.

CHAPTER SIXTEEN

EQUATOR

June 26th we crossed the equator at Latitude 00000, Longitude 165-59-01 degrees. All of the

Polywogs who had not been across the equator before were duly initiated by the "Shellbacks". The "Shellbacks" are those who had crossed the equator previously.

It wasn't really a pleasant experience to the Polywogs, rather a childish event, but the Shellbacks seemed to enjoy it.

Now we were members of the "Ancient Order of the Deep" and privileged to the "Solemn Mysteries of the Ancient Order". Next time it would be our turn to do the initiating.

Around the Equator a Jap Cruiser and a couple of destroyers were picked up on Radar. We screwed the governors down and out ran them. We didn't want a fight with them. With all the fuel and ammunition we had on board, they would have blown us out of the water. We would have all ended up in "Davy Jones Locker."

Initiation of the Shellback's, those sailors crossing the Equator for the first time.

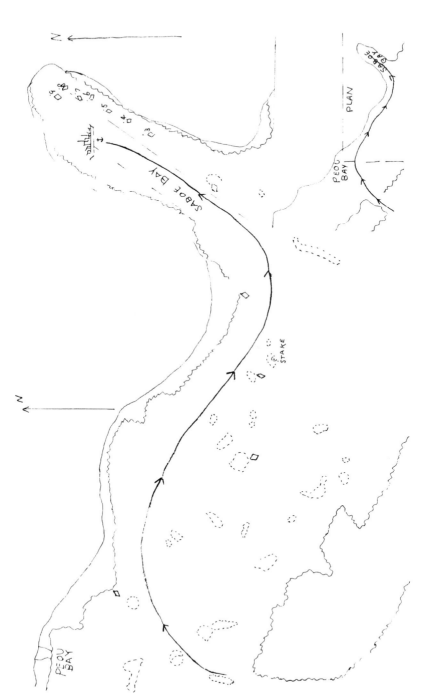

N

N

SABOE BAY

PEOU
BAY

PEOU
BAY

STAKE

SABOE
BAY

SABOE BAY

PEOU
PLAN

Vanikoro Island, Santa Cruz Islands

CHAPTER SEVENTEEN

SABOE BAY, SANTA CRUZ ISLANDS

We left the Marines at Espiritu and went on to the Santa Cruz Islands. There was a harbor there called Saboe Bay, Vanikoro Island.

We arrived there about July 6th, the day before my 19th birthday. We were to relieve the USS Mackinac, a sister ship, that had been there for several months without incident.

We were there for the purpose of carrying out seaplane tending operations. The work proceeded without any problems until July 14th. Contacts were made with Japanese planes.

On the evening of the fifteenth, the crew was watching a movie on the fantail of the ship. It was a beautiful evening and pleasant to be relaxing. Everything quiet until a plane was heard in the distance. As it got nearer to us we realized it was a Japanese reconnaissance plane. He dropped enough flares to light us up like a Christmas tree. We assume he took pictures so they could prepare to attack us.

CHAPTER EIGHTEEN

PREPARE FOR ATTACK

"All Hands, General Quarters" was sounded. All men went to their battle stations and the crew of the Chincoteague stood ready for any attack.

The belief was that the Japanese did not plan to attack until morning. Approximately twelve PBY's needed to be serviced in the morning so work would get under way as early as possible.

There were two fifty-foot Motor Whale Boats and two forty-feet Motor Launches equipped with fuel tanks and supplies to service the PBY's. Each was assigned two crews and worked alternate days.

On the morning of the sixteenth, just after 7 am , five Japanese bombers made a bombing run. They released their bombs at an altitude of 8,000 feet and then left. The bombs landed in the jungle. Four hours later nine bombers were sighted. At that time the Chinc

PBY Patrol Bomber, the type of plane service by the USS Chincoteague.

immediately got underway and headed for the open sea. The same group came over for a second run, dropping bombs which fell fifty yards from the stern. There was
minor damage from bomb fragments.

As the ship was entering the sea from the mouth of the Bay, a third attack came. Two bombs landed in

Empty powder cases from a 5 inch gun.

the water fifty feet from the starboard side. The bombs detonated below the surface of the water and made

many shrapnel holes above and below the water line.

The interior structure was damaged, and

40mm. gun being fired from the deck of the USS Chincoteague.

started fires in two aviation crew sleeping compartments. These were quickly extinguished by a sprinkler system, but minor flooding developed.

The gasoline lines were also ruptures and caught fire at the fueling station, but the gasoline tanks were not ruptured and the damage control party soon had the fire under control.

Some of the holes were plugged and a canvas was used to cover some of them. This was not very effective, but certainly helped some.

PBY bomber, an amphibious plane flown during WW11.

A small general purpose bomb with a delayed action fuse penetrated the superstructure, main the second decks and detonated in the after engine room.

Another bomb dropped about fifteen feet from the port side and detonated under water. It did not pierce the ship, but the explosion caused a shock that stopped the forward engines. CHINCOTEAGUE WAS DEAD IN THE WATER.

Repairs were made, the engines started, and she was under way again. Chincoteague returned to the Bay.

All was quiet during the night. The next morning the bomber group returned from its mission and landed. The last plane landed about 0730, and the Chincoteague was immediately in a bombing attack from five enemy twin-engined bombers. They had followed the patrol bombers. Again, we were driven out of the Bay.

Every day for the next couple of days, the Japanese bombers would come back and drop bombs and drive our ship out of the bay into the open sea.

The radio man, Freidman, was asked to contact communications for fighter protection. Word came in that there was a big fight going on some where else and none were available to help us. We'd have to take care of ourselves. Maybe we would get out to sea before they came back to attack us again.

I can still remember those bombs coming out of those bomb bays. They looked like little capsules when they first started out at about 30,000 feet. They got bigger and bigger as they got closer and closer. The screaming of those bombs scared me so bad that to this day I hate the sound of sirens and screaming fireworks. Fortunately, they were still landing mostly in the harbor and the jungle.

When the nine bombers came for their attack it was our first real practice shooting at the enemy planes. They were coming in low, maybe we could hit one.

We were warned that we would have to work fast if we were hit. There was so much high-octane fuel, bombs, and torpedoes on the ship, that we would go up like a torch.

The nine bombers that came over didn't drop any

bombs. They were sizing us up for the kill. Everybody, remain alert the captain warned, they'll be back and they'll let us have it the next time.

The Captain was certain we would be attacked again. He also felt it was our duty to go back into the harbor to service the seaplanes so they could continue their patrol missions.

The gallant Chincoteague returned to the harbor and her job to refuel the seaplanes.

CHAPTER NINETEEN

ANOTHER DAY

Night brought a protective covering of darkness to our ship, and a few hours of reprieve, but we knew the enemy would be back, so our rest was uneasy.

With the dawn came another wave of Japanese Bombers, and then yet another wave of bombers. They were determined to sink the Chincoteague.

The Captain said if we stayed in the harbor we'd be sunk for sure. He gave orders to slip the anchor and head for the sea.

The four fueling crews were ordered to get in the launches and continue fueling the seaplanes. On this day I was ordered to go with them. This wasn't my

Sick bay established on deck to treat the crew wounded during the bombings.

normal duty, but you do as you are told.

When the Chinc slipped anchor and started pulling away, the Captain shouted to us that they would be back to get us if they could. They didn't come back.

The courageous little Chincoteague was attacked three times before it could reach the mouth of the harbor. That made four attacks and she was still afloat.

CHAPTER TWENTY

FIRST SERIOUS DAMAGE

The first serious damage occurred in the fifth attack. A fire started in a lower compartment, gas lines ruptured, and the fire couldn't be put out. This was very serious. The gas valves had been jarred open and the damage control crew couldn't get to them.

The Navigator said he knew where the valves were and he would like to try to get to them to shut

Mess compartment damaged during bombings.

them off. It seemed the only chance to save the ship, so Captain Hobbs gave his okay.

Down in the hold of the ship, in darkness, among the tanks and pipes and valves, Wilson, Whittington and Horman made their way to the open valves. He was able to reach them. They pumped the system and closed the valves.

It was a long wait for them to return. A slight error could have blown the Chincoteague to Kingdom Come.

At last he came back, reported that he had reached the valves and was able to close them. Now the fire could be brought under control.

This danger over, the Captain thought he must return to the Harbor. The seaplanes needed their supplies.

Following behind and ready for the kill, came the Japanese bombers. For the sixth time, bombs were dropping around the Chincoteague. Now she was being hit.

All but three planes had been serviced, when the Captain said they had better return to sea again. It was getting too dangerous where we were.

The Chinc reeled from the sixth attack, recovered and went on, then came the seventh and the eighth attack.

Five of them were coming in low, right out of the sun. It was impossible for the gunners to see them. They were dropping bombs and the Chincoteague received a direct hit on the afterdeck. It was a delayed action bomb and it knocked out the after engine room. There was on power out of there.

Ten men were killed in this attack. One in the Mess compartment and nine in the engine room.

CHAPTER TWENTY-ONE

HEAVY DAMAGE

This attack had been a bad one. Most of the life boats were damaged and un-usable. The hull was full of splinters, and there was some fire below decks. One engine room was out of commission, but she was still afloat. No one was sure how she had survived all these bombing raids, and was still afloat.

The enemy seemed determined to sink our ship, and the crew was just as determined to save her. This was our home and we didn't like somebody messing around with it.

My gun crew from #3 gun (5-inch, .38-Caliber).

CHAPTER TWENTY-TWO

DEAD IN THE WATER

The next attack brought paralyzing damage to the Chinc. A near miss put the forward engine room out of commission. Now she was dead in the water, without power, without pumps, without lights and it was late in the day. It would soon be dark.

Captain Hobbs had a very tough decision to make. There was danger of an explosion, but there were few life boats. Most of them had been destroyed. Also, the sharks were swimming around and around the ship waiting for a good meal, which they hoped would be the men on board.

The order to abandon ship was not given. Then came the bad news. The forward engine room was flooding. Work had to be stopped on the engines. Somehow the water had to be kept down so the work could continue. The Captain ordered every man, including the gun crews to form a bucket brigade.

Everyone who was able to grab a bucket and were filling and passing from man to man, to be emptied back into the ocean. The chanting "Heave Ho . . Heave Ho . ." could be heard coming from the depths of the ship.

The deck was read hot from the fire burning in the engine room. It was like walking over hell, and it was a wonder anyone was able to do it.

The flooding was being controlled, but it couldn't be stopped. Captain Hobbs gave orders to throw all the heavy gear that wasn't absolutely essential overboard.

The pumps couldn't handle the flooding, the bucket brigade was doing their best, but the Chinc was sinking. Two feet from the top of the deck to the ocean, but she was still afloat, although she was listing badly.

Captain Hobbs still did not want to give the order to abandon ship, although it looked like something had to be done to save the lives of the crew.

CHAPTER TWENTY-THREE

HELP WAS COMING

While he was discussing this with another officer, they suddenly heard a plane in the distance. It didn't sound like a Japanese plane. They were hoping it was help coming.

It was! It was a PBY and they knew it would have pumps on board. The Commodore had ordered them to be brought out to the Chincoteague. Hopefully, they thought, they were sending fighter planes, too. Maybe there would be some fighter planes if the enemy came back in the afternoon.

She wouldn't go down those last two feet. The pumps would keep her afloat until the fighters came.

The Thornton, another seaplane tender, returned from a depth-charge attack on an enemy submarine, came along side to offer assistance.

Army plane coming in to see if we were still afloat.

Burn victim being lifted by crane to a motor launch to be taken to a hospital.

Burn victims being transported by motor launch to a PBY plane to be taken
to Espiritu Santo Hospital.

CHAPTER TWENTY-FOUR

THE ELEVENTH ATTACK

At sunset, the eleventh attack came. The Commander of the Thornton said they would stay along side to give all the help possible. He was putting his ship in danger, but insisted they would stay. The Chincoteague would need all the help she could get.

She was listing eighteen degrees and had suffered all the damage she could take. Then as a wave of Japanese bombers were coming in for the kill, over them like guardian angels came Marine Corsairs.

CHAPTER TWENTY-FIVE

WHISTLING DEATH

There were four of them. The Japs saw them too, and they turned and starting jettisoning their bombs in the ocean. They were trying to lighten up so they would have a better chance of getting away.

Two of the enemy planes were in flames and going down. Then another Corsair came and got another Japanese plane trying to get away. The Japanese called the Corsairs "Whistling Death" because of the sound they made. The Marines were our Angels in disguise.

The Chincoteague would survive. Badly damaged, but still afloat.

CHAPTER TWENTY-SIX

BURIAL AT SEA

All enlisted personnel, except for the gun crew, were transferred to the Thornton. The ship was in danger and this was a safer place to be.

All personnel and officers who could be spared from "repair parties and bucket brigades" were called to quarters on the port side of the boat deck. Commander Hobbs officiated at the funeral services for the sailor killed in one of the attacks. He was buried at sea with full military honors.

Nine more casualties were still entombed in the engine room. They could not be moved yet, as fires were still burning and the heat was extreme.

CHAPTER TWENTY-SEVEN

THE CHINCOTEAGUE IS SAVED

Commander Hobbs and the entire crew were elated that their ship, the Chincoteague had been saved. There was also deep sadness and mourning for the ten who had perished.

The Chincoteague sat dead in the water for three days, sixty hours of that time the crew had manned the bucket brigade, but there was a deep feeling of accomplishment and thankfulness.

Group picture of USS Chincoteague crew. Commander Hobbs is the officer with the binoculars around his neck on the right.

CHAPTER TWENTY-EIGHT

FIFTEEN MEN RETURNED

July 19, 1943, according to the ships' logs: "H.F. Benson, First Class Petty Officer and fifteen men returned aboard from USS Sonoma." Nothing is said about where we were and why we were there.

We had our own story to tell from our experience being left in the launches while the Chinc went out to sea, trying to dodge Japanese bombs. Commander Hobbs said they would return for us if possible, but they never did. She was disabled, and not able to come back. We thought she had been sunk.

At the time of the last Japanese attack, there were about twelve PBY seaplanes moored at bouys in the Bay. The crews in the boats transported all of the plane crewmen to their planes and fueled them as needed. All of the planes got off the water.

After the planes were airborne, the crews in the boats went to shore, dropped anchors overboard, abandoned the boats and waded to shore.

We were still hoping our ship would return for us, but after three or four days, we gave up.

The enemy planes were flying over us all the time and dropping bombs. I was very frightened. I found a huge tree with a fork in the roots and I hid in that. This experience was so traumatic that a lot of it was erased from my memory. With this research and writing, it is coming back to me.

There were friendly natives on the island. There were running around with their Bolo knives, looking for the Japanese. When planes came over, we could tell if they were friend or enemy by the way the natives reacted. If they started to run, we knew they were enemy.

At the other end of the island there was a dock and the home of an English Overseer. I believe there was some sort of Officers Club. We congregated there. We ate a lot of bananas and coconuts.

Finally, we decided we would have to figure out what we were going to do. We had given up hope that the Chinc was going to return for us. On the chance that she might still be afloat, we decided we should look for her.

It was either that or sit there and wait to be rescued or to be captured by the Japanese. This didn't seem like anything we were looking forward to. We were between "the Devil and the Deep Blue Sea", and chose the sea. We had only one .45-caliber side arm for sixteen of us and no other way to defend ourselves.

There was an old crane left by an English company that had used it for logging Ironwood. We steamed it up and took a 500 gallon fuel tank out of one of the fifty-foot motor launches. We then gathered all the drums of diesel fuel and loaded them into the launch. We loaded all the food rations and filled the water casks with fresh water.

When we were ready to leave, we sank the three remaining boats so the enemy couldn't use them to come after us. We sank them by taking the plugs out of the bottom, so they could be salvaged if we had to come back.

CHAPTER TWENTY-NINE

MIDNIGHT

We left the island at midnight, using a boat hook to feel our way through the channel. There was only one narrow channel and we had to be sure not to get hung up on the reefs.

We made it from the lagoon out through the channel without too much trouble. We went seventy-two miles out into the open sea and were out there

I was on this 50-foot motor launch searching for the Chincoteague after being left on Vanikoro Island.

eighteen hours before we were rescued.

We spotted a large plane flying toward us. We didn't know if it was friendly or an enemy plane. We were flying our American flag and he signaled us by blinker. One of the shipmates was a signalman and he returned a message. A few hours later we were spotted by a tug boat, the Sonoma, that was looking for the Chincoteague. They told us they had heard it had been sunk and were looking for survivors. They took us aboard and fed us a very welcome meal.

A short time later, the Chinc was spotted and she looked like she was ready to sink. She had an eighteen degree list and no power.

The tug boat, the USS Sonoma, took her under tow. We were transferred back to our ship on July 19th.

Heavy seas forced the Thornton to cast off on the morning of July 19th. Not long after the tug, Sonoma AT12, came alongside with additional pumping equipment and took Chincoteague in tow. We arrived at Espiritu Santo on the morning of July 21.

CHAPTER THIRTY

REPAIRS

We went along side the destroyer tender The USS Dixie for minor repairs. The hull was made watertight,, the water pumped out. It was repaired good enough to be towed to Mare Island Navy Yard, California for major repairs.

July 22, 1943, the bodies of the nine men were removed from the after engine room. I was asked to help with this detail, but asked them to please not make me do that. I guess they felt a little compassion at this time and I was excused from this duty. Funeral services were held at 0930 on the morning of the 23rd.

The burial notice had a postscript stating, "This message as a result of being bombed to a standstill on 17 July, 1943, in the vicinity of Espiritu Santo, New Hebrides, South Pacific. Ship bombed so badly that twice was given up for lost, but through the efforts of all hands, was brought safely into harbor." The message was sent from the Chincoteague to Commander Fleet Air Wing.

CHAPTER THIRTY-ONE

BACK TO THE STATES

August 3, we began taking on supplies, stores, life boats, medical supplies in preparation for being towed back to the States. August 10, she was on her way home.

She was towed to San Francisco by a US tug. Every time there was a submarine scare, which was quite often, the tug would cut loose and run, leaving the Chinc to the mercy of the enemy. It took almost a month to cross the ocean.

One third of the crew returned aboard the Chinc. The rest of us were sent back on a Dutch transport. The Japara was formerly a luxury liner.

The first thing when we came on board was to be assigned to our quarters. We were required to wear our white uniforms. For the entire trip we were fed beans. Beans in the morning; beans and vienna sausage at noon; beans and spam for dinner. I guess they had lots of beans because that's what they fed us for three weeks.

When we got to Treasure Island, we were given a T-Bone steak dinner. That was the best T-Bone I ever had! We were all given a ten day leave and then some of us were re-assigned to other ships.

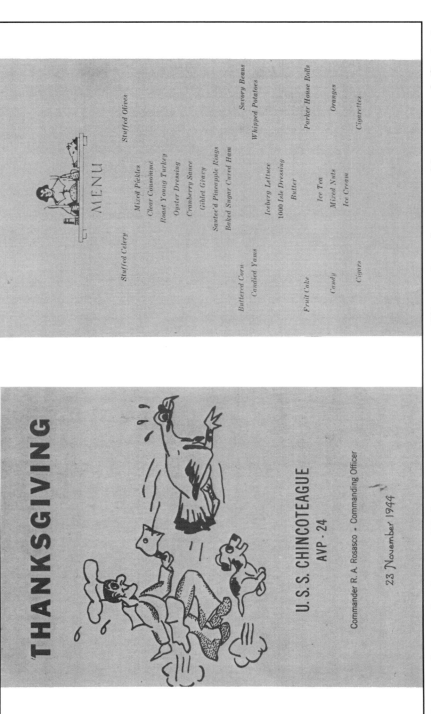

Thanksgiving Dinner menu offer in Iwo Jima, 1944.

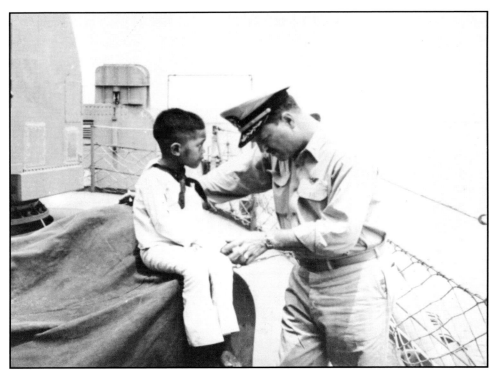

Captain Rosasco with one of the few natives to survive on Parry Atoll Enivetok.
February, 1944
The boy was wounded by shrapnel and later returned to the island.

CHAPTER THIRTY-TWO

THE CHINCOTEAGUE STILL LIVES

The Chincoteague story doesn't end here. She put out for Pearl Harbor in January, 1944. She saw duty in the Solomons, the occupation of the Marshalls, the Treasuries, Kwajalein, Mariana's, New Hebrides, Iwo Jima and Enewetok. She escorted a convoy back to

The USS Chincoteague's first birthday.

Pearl Harbor. She also went to Guam, Okinawa, the Palaus, Tsingtoa, China and Ulithe.

In February, 1944, she went to Iwo Jima and tended seaplanes there during that assault. She tended seaplanes at Ulithi and then went back in for another overhaul.

Joining the occupation forces, she tended seaplanes at Okinawa and Tsingtoa, China until March of 1946.

The USS Chincoteague

THIRTY-THREE

TYPHOON

The following is quoted from a letter written to be by Richard Fales: "I was a latter-day-crewman on the Chincoteague, and was the mailman (Mam 3/c). I joined the ship shortly after Christmas in 1945 in Tsingtoa, China. Shortly thereafter we assumed the Seadrome in Shanghai on the Whangpoo River. It was a lot better than the cold and bleak part of North China we had left.

Just about the time a lot of us had accumulated enough points to get back home in the Spring of 1946, it was announced that we were frozen, as we were going to a place called Bikini to set up a Seadrome for

Group picture of the crew on the deck of the Chincoteague.

the upcoming atomic tests.

Without our relatively short fuel supply, we went first to Saipan, then departed the next day for our new assignment.

Since sailors of the US Navy are not allowed to drink alcohol on board ship, they use "Beer Raft", set afloat away from the ship so the crew could have a beer once in a wh[...]

The weather dictated otherwise. We ran smack into a typhoon. It's a good thing I was young. At my age today, I probably would have died from fright, rather than thinking it was a marvelous and exciting experience.

We got battered for the better part of three days, and finally limped into Midway (Hardly the most direct route from Saipan to Bikini!). To illustrate the severity of the storm, as we wallowed in troughs, the fore and aft five inchers were under water alternately. The pounding of the waves crushed the splinter shields on both sides of Officer Country, narrowing the remaining passages to less than two feet. Our Bikini assignment was obviously cancelled and we headed back stateside to Long Beach and San Pedro for repairs then to Pier 99, San Diego, thence through the Panama Canal to New Orleans, and then to Beaumont, Texas. That's where I kissed her goodbye!"

This in itself was another brilliant experience for the Chincoteague, but this ship was not ready for retirement. Many of my fellow shipmates thought she had been scrapped. But this did not happen.

CHAPTER THIRTY-FOUR

THE COAST GUARD

In March of 1949, the Chincoteague, was lent to the Coast Guard and was given the hull number WAVP 375. She was refurbished to some extent with the removal of some of the guns.

She also did some heroic work while with the Coast Guard. She was assigned to North Atlantic Weather Patrol. While on this duty, at times, became covered with unbelievable amounts of ice. It seems like she would have sunk from the weight of it.

In a letter from a retired Captain in the Coast Guard, he stated he served on the Chinc from June, 1954, to September, 1957, while she was home based at Norfolk, Virginia. This is quoted from his letter, "Our mission in those years was ocean station patrols (weather station) in the North Atlantic and search and rescue. I made fourteen such patrols. The winters in the North Atlantic, of course, provides some awesome sea conditions. I remember many days of testing the Chincoteague's hull strength as she would come out of the water while going over huge waves and then slam back into the sea against her very flat midship bottom shape."

He further says, "To this day, I can tell you I was and still am impressed at the commitment of your shipmates in bringing the Chincoteague back to Pearl Harbor and Mare Island."

The Chincoteague saw continuous service with the Coast Guard into the 1970's. In 1970, she sailed on a cadet training cruise. In June, 1972, she was

USS Chincoteague, under the Golden Gate Bridge, San Francisco, California.

North Atlantic Weather Patrol while under commission for the Coast Guard.

ployed with the Coast Guard personnel to the South Vietnamese Government and renamed Ly Thoung Kiet HQ-16. She remained there until the government fell in 1975. Then she left the country.

The Chincoteague is still seeing service in the Philippine Navy. She is being used as an auxiliary ship and has been renamed "Andress Banifaco 7".

The Chincoteague AVP 24 was a wonderful ship and it seem everyone who sailed aboard her has a special place in their hearts for her. Commander Hobbs said she was "A mighty rugged seagoing ship."

CHAPTER THIRTY-FIVE

TYPES OF BOMBS

The United States Navy Bomb Disposal School identified the bomb which struck the Chincoteague from fragments recovered. The one which directly hit her was a Japanese type 99, No. 6, with a total weight of 136.4 pounds and contained an explosive charge of 70.4 pounds of Picric Acid. It was a semi-armor piercing bomb. The bomb passed through three decks totaling 13/16 inches in thickness. It had a short duration fuse and detonated 25 to 30 feet from point of impact.

Bombs number two and three were probably the same. They landed a short distance from the starboard side and exploded under water.

Bomb number four detonated below the surface of the water about thirty feet from the port shell of the vessel. It estimated to have been a 500 pound bomb.

About 663 tons of water were taken aboard as a result of the direct hit. The corresponding displacement was about 3,721 tons. The vessel assumed a starboard list, variously reported as twelve to eighteen degrees, putting the main deck edge a few inches above water.

In spite of heavy damage and flooding, the Chincoteague's personnel succeeded in saving their ship. This achievement is all the more remarkable in view of the comparative inexperience of the crew. Only about a month had elapsed from the time the ship left San Diego upon completion of post shakedown repairs, until this action occurred.

THIS EXPERIENCE WAS ENOUGH TO LAST US A LIFETIME!

View of port side, showing locations of bombs.

Fragment holes resulting from bomb No. 1. Note torn degaussing cables and buckled beam brackets.

Fragment holes and water column.

Location of initial impact of direct hit, bomb No. 3.

Path of direct hit bomb No. 3 through
superstructure and main decks.

Path of direct hit bomb No. 3 through main and second
decks.   Note buckled deck and bulkheads due to
detonation in engine room below.

Path of direct hit bomb No. 3 in after engine room.

CHAPTER THIRTY-SIX

LIFE AFTER THE NAVY

I served on two other ships during and after
World War Two. After being discharged, I returned to
North Dakota and went to work for the Great Northern
Railroad.

I met my future wife there and we were married
in 1951. We have one son, Karl. He has worked for
the Burlington Northern for twenty years. He is
married and he and his wife, Patti, have two children,
Thomas and Tina.

My last years on the railroad were working out
of Vancouver, Washington, and Portland, Oregon. I
worked as a Brakeman and Conductor on Amtrak,
going to Spokane, Washington. I enjoyed the contact
with people who were traveling.

I retired in 1986.

Frank and Carol Murphy

APPENDIX A

Name_____ Murphy, Francis D._____
(Name in Full, Surname to the Left)

5546408 _____ Rate _S 2/c_ USN.
(Service No.)

Date Reported Aboard: April 12, 1943.

____U.S.S. CHINCOTEAGUE(AVP24).
(Present Ship or Station)

HOUGHTON, WASHINGTON
(Ship or Station Received From)

8-10-43: Served on board with distinction during repeated bombing attacks with resultant casualties, fires, flooding, loss of light and power, July 16-21, 1943 and for bringing ship to port for which the Officers and Crew were commended by Commander Fleet Air Wing ONE.

I. E. HOBBS, Commander, U. S. Navy.

Commendation given to Frank Murphy for his performance on board the USS Chincoteague during the repeated bombings by the Japanese.

The crew of the USS Chincoteague receiving their Purple Heart medals for
bravery during the Japanese bombings.

APPENDIX B

Actual report made by the US Navy regarding the injuries and deaths aboard the USS Chincoteague during the Japanese bombings.

UNITED STATES SHIP ___CHINCOTEAGUE___ Saturday, 17 JULY, 19 43
(Day) (Date) (Month)

ZONE DESCRIPTION ___-11___   REMARKS.

0-4 No remarks

W.B. WILSON, Lieut., USNR.

4-8 0738 The following named men suffered severe burns from bomb flash, gasoline fire and shrapnel wounds as indicated: STARRATT, Kenneth Malcom, RM2c, USN, entire body from waist up badly burned; DRISKELL, James Hermon, F2c, V-6, USNR, entire body from waist up badly burned; COLEMAN, C.H., 623-94-01, AMM3c, V-6, USNR, received shrapnel wound in right leg and in back.

W.B. WILSON, Lieut., USNR.

8-12 1000 Transferred above named men to PBY plane for further transfer to Naval Hospital Expiritu Santo for further treatment. - McNELEY, Richard Bannister, PhM1c, accompanied patients in plane as medical representative. Records and accounts retained aboard.

W.B. WILSON, Lieut., USNR.

12-16 1200 Bomb exploded in after engine room killing following personnel: Lieutenant (jg) Percy Alton WEAVER, E-V(G), USNR; BERRY, Carey Woodson, 274-28-47, CMM(PA), USN; GOBBLE, Carl Smith, jr., 266-10-40, MoMM1c, USN; CLOTFELTER, Chester William, 283-24-02, MoMM1c, USN; CREEDEN, Harold James, 201-89-81, MoMM2c, USN; HARP, John William, 564-16-58, F2c, V-6, USNR; HEBERT, Jennings Placide, 645-21-29, MoMM2c, V-6, USNR; GOODMAN, Carl Irving, 385-87-06, EM2c, USN. The following named was killed at the same time in forward messing compartment directly above after engine room: STROUD, Herschel Eugene, 669-62-54, F2c, V-6, USNR. Due to the after engine room being completely flooded, these bodies could not be recovered at this time. The following injuries to personnel have been sustained: WALRAVEN, Harry J., S2c, knocked off trainers stand by concussion, possible fracture elbow and forearm; SADLOCHA, TM2c, shrapnel in leg; CAMPBELL, R.E., CM1c, shock; RIORDAN, Raymond E. CPhM(PA), shock; STULGIS, Charles A., CMM(PA), shock; LYON, Herbert R., MoMM1c, M-2, USNR, shock and bruises; WISNEWSKI, John Anthony, CMoMM(AA), shock; DANE, Joseph Howard, F1c, USN, shock; CHRZANOWSKI, Stanley, Cox, USN, shrapnel in right arm. During bombing numerous minor injuries to personnel sustained, each was given medical attention.

W.B. WILSON, Lieut., USNR.

-20 No remarks

W.B. WILSON, Lieut., USNR.

20-24 No remarks

W.B. WILSON, Lieut., USNR.

Approved: Examined:

U.S. N. Navigator.

UNITED STATES SHIP ___CHINCOTEAGUE___   Sunday (Day) __18__ (Date) __July__ (Month) , 19 43

ZONE DESCRIPTION ___-11___   **REMARKS.**

0-4   No remarks
W. B. WILSON, Lieut., USNR.

4-8   0600 All CHINCOTEAGUE enlisted personnel with exception of 5"/38 gun crews and repair party men were transferred to USS THORNTON.
W. B. WILSON, Lieut., USNR.

8-12   No remarks
W. B. WILSON, Lieut., USNR.

12-16 1310 Following named men transferred aboard PBY to be rushed to Naval Hospital, Espiritu Santo for treatment of shock: WISNEWSKI, John Anthony, CMOMM(AA), USN; BANE, Joseph Howard, F1c, USN.
W. B. WILSLN, Lieut., USNR.

16-20 1630 All CHINCOTEAGUE personnel returned aboard ship. 1840 All personnel and officers who could be spared from repair parties and bucket brigades were called to quarters on port side of boat deck. Commanding Officer officiated at funeral services for STROUD, Herschel Eugene, 669-62-54, F2c, V-6, USNR. 1853 STROUD was buried at sea.
W. B. WILSON, Lieut., USNR.

20-24 No remarks
W. B. WILSON, Lieut., USNR.

Approved:
J Earl Slable

Examined:
W. B. Wilson
Lt. U. S. N. R., Navigator.

UNITED STATES SHIP CHINCOTEAGUE   Monday 19 July, 1943

ZONE DESCRIPTION -11   **REMARKS.**

0-4   No remarks

W.B. Wilson
W.B. WILSON, Lieut., USNR.

4-8   No remarks

W.B. Wilson
W.B. WILSON, Lieut., USNR.

8-12   1113 H.F., BENSON, CQM and 15 men returned aboard from U.S.S. SONOMA.

W.B. Wilson
W.B. WILSON, Lieut., USNR.

12-16   No remarks

W.B. Wilson
W.B. WILSON, Lieut., USNR.

16-20   1700 Held General Muster. Found no men missing.

W.P. Brennan
W.P. BRENNAN, Ens., USNR.

20-24   No remarks

D.E. Holland
D.E. HOLLAND, Bos'n, USN.

Approved: Examined:

(signature)   *W.B. Wilson*
                             U.S.N. Navigator.

APPENDIX C

Excerpts from the official "BOMB DAMAGE" report, U.S.S. CHINCOTEAGUE (AVP24), SABOE BAY, SANTA CRUZ ISLANDS, July 17, 1943. This report is dated September 20, 1944 and was generated from the Preliminary Design Section, Bureau of Ships, Navy Department, War Damage Report No. 47.

U.S.S. CHINCOTEAGUE (AVP24)

Bomb Damage

Saboe Bay, Santa Cruz Islands
17 July, 1943

Class..........Seaplane Tender
Small (AVP10)

Launched..........April 15, 1942

Displacement..........1,695 Tons

Length (W.L.)..........300 Ft. 0 In.

Beam (W.L.)..........41 Ft. 1 In.

Draft (Before Damage)
Forward..........12 Ft. 0 In.
Aft..........14 Ft. 7 In.

SECTION I - SUMMARY

1.   CHINCOTEAGUE underwent eleven bombing attacks on 16-17 July, 1943, while on a seaplane tending mission in the Santa Cruz Islands. The attacking groups varied from a single plane to a formation of nine bombers. CHINCOTEAGUE'S survival is attributable both to the aggressive manner in which her personnel took action to remove the damage water and to her adequate stability characteristics.

5.   At 0245, on 18 July, the inboard one of the two main propulsion diesels in the forward engine room overheated, and in an attempt to secure the engine, control was lost and the engine ran away, driving the crew from the engine room and starting a serious fire. The fire was confined to the engine room and gradually burned itself out.

7.   The condition of negative stability was the result of free surface caused by:

(a) Free water remaining from the first attack.

(b) Water on the second deck which entered after the direct hit through holes ineffectively plugged after the first attack.

(c) Flooding incident to the direct hit.

14.   Cofferdam C-6V flooded to the waterline through fragment holes. All compartments in the

refrigerator space on the platform deck between bulkheads 113 and 121, except the meat room, flooded to a depth of four (4) feet through fragment holes in the shell below the second deck. This flooding was eliminated by opening manholes in the platform deck and allowing the water to enter stuffing box compartments C-414E and C-413E from which it was pumped overboard by the ship's drainage system. Aviation lubricating oil pump room C-415E flooded to the overhead through open watertight access hatch 3-117-1 on the platform deck. Fragment holes below the second deck were plugged.

15.   As a result of the bomb (No. 2 on Plate 1) detonating opposite frame 54 starboard, numerous fragments dented and pierced the shell of the vessel. Little interior damage was noted. The column of water caused by the bomb detonation deluged the topsides and buckled the 1/4-inch STS splinter protection bulwark on the main deck in way of the torpedo stowage. Hot fragments ignited on the starboard motor whaleboat. The fire was extinguished quickly. Water entered all starboard compartments between bulkheads 44 and 65 on the platform deck through fragment holes in the shell. The armory (A-310-1A) flooded to a depth of 2 feet 6 inches. Water traveled athwartships through non-watertight doors, flooding the passageway and S.D. stores A-310-1A on the port side to about the same depth. Torpedo workshop A-310-1AE flooded to a depth of one foot. The water in these compartments was eventually cleared by plugging the fragment holes and using submersible pumps and bucket brigades. In

S.D. stores A-310-1A, many loose papers hampered the unwatering process by intermittently clogging the strainers of the submersible pumps. 20mm clipping room A-308M and 20mm magazine A-309M also flooded to a depth of one foot. Fragment holes in these compartments were plugged and the water removed by a bucket brigade. As reported in reference (f), small arms magazine A-307M flooded to the waterline through fragment holes. Underwater sound room A-421C flooded completely through watertight hatch 3-59-1 in passageway A-310-1A, which was not properly secured. These two compartments were not unwatered until drydocking. The fragment holes in aviation bunk room A-207-1L on the second deck above the waterline, wee not plugged properly and resulted in some flooding during later attacks when a list developed.

17.   Five minutes later, a second attack developed. In this attack, the vessel was struck by a small general purpose bomb with a short delay in the fuze. The bomb pierced the superstructure deck between frames 81 and 82 about 18 inches inboard of the port deck edge, and continued through the main and second decks, traveling almost vertically downward and slightly inboard. After piercing the second deck, the bomb was deflected aft by bulkhead 81 and detonated in the after engine room at about frame 84, just forward of and between the two diesel main engines. The inner bottom was ruptured, but the shell of the vessel was not pierced. Foundations and piping in the vicinity of the detonation were demolished. An 8-inch suction

line, supplying cooling water to the main propulsion diesel engines was ruptured. The engine room flooded to the overhead. The port side of bulkhead 81 was badly buckled and ruptured and bulkhead 80 was distorted and punctured. The second deck above the engine room was bulged up a maximum of 16 inches over the detonation were demolished. An 8-inch suction line, supplying cooling water to the main propulsion diesel engines was ruptured. The engine room flooded to the overhead. The port side of bulkhead 81 was badly buckled and ruptured and bulkhead 80 was distorted and punctured. The second deck above the engine room was bulged up a maximum of 16 inches over the detonation. Other effects of the blast were noted in damaged access and ventilation trunks. The rapid flooding of the after engine room and other material damage resulted in loss of power to the port shaft and rendered useless other important auxiliaries. CHINCOTEAGUE remained at sea following this attack, maintaining a sped of 10 knots by the forward engines. The flooding resulting from No. 3 bomb caused the vessel to settle and trim by the stern, placing the second deck aft of amidships below the waterline. Compartments C-201L and C-202L began to flood slowly through the ineffectively plugged fragment holes. This flooding reduced the stability of CHINCOTEAGUE in a negative value and a list to starboard developed. This resulted in increased flooding in C-201L and C-202L and caused water to enter aviation bunk room A-207-1L.

18.   At 1420, of the same afternoon, three bombers dropped numerous bombs which bracketed the ship.

One bomb detonated about 15 feet from the port side of frame 65. The detonation dented a large area of shell plating between 54 and 74. The plating was neither ruptured nor pierced by fragments. The main area of indentation extended from about 2 feet above the waterline to about 5 feet below with less indentation extending up to the main deck. The column of water also deluged the topside, doing damage to equipment. Shock broke electrical equipment and gages in the forward engine room. At this point, the forward main engines stopped, leaving CHINCOTEAGUE dead in the water.

19.   At 1450, with CHINCOTEAGUE dead in the water, a single plane made another attack. No damage resulted, as the bombs fell about 200 yards abeam. At about 1800, the eleventh and final attack was made, but the enemy planes were driven off by air cover which had been provided in the meantime.
CHINCOTEAGUE at this point had lost all power, was flooding slowly in many compartments, and was listing to starboard.

22.   At 0230, on 18 July, the inboard (No. 2) main engines began to overheat and black smoke was emitted from the stack. At 0245, in was decided to investigate the engine. It was not desirable to stop both main engines simultaneously since all starting air had been exhausted and it would have been impossible to restart them. the procedure followed in picking up the THORNTON small boat two hours previously, had been to place the engines in idling position and then

dump the oil from the hydraulic clutch, thus taking power off the propeller shaft. The same procedure was followed in investigating the overheating of No. 2 engine. When the load was removed, however, the engine began to speed up. The throttle was closed with no apparent effect. No 2 engine picked up speed rapidly and within 30 seconds, had reached a dangerously high speed. No. 1 engine was secured, and the engine room abandoned with No. 2 engine racing out of control. The runaway engine started a fire. An effort was made to smother the fire by closing all access openings and at the same time foam generators were set up. THORNTON came alongside, hoses were connected to her fire mains and foam poured into the compartment. The fire was fought until 0545, when the last of the foam was expended. The compartment was then battened down and all intakes plugged. The fire at this time appeared to be localized, but still smoldering. The after bulkhead of I.C. Room A-310-2C was kept cool by spray from a gasoline handy billy pump.

23.   At 0740, the tow line was broken because of a submarine contact. THORNTON resumed the tow at 0939 and continued until 1217, at which time the list had increased to a point where the tow had to be dropped. Flooding continued to gain despite the efforts of the crew. The stern had settled and the list was variously reported as 12 to 18 degrees starboard. Orders were given to lighten ship. Torpedoes, heavy machinery, winches and other gear on the starboard side were jettisoned. Apparently, as the result of a

radio request to Espiritu Santo, additional pumps were flown in by a patrol plane. These eventually removed much of the free surface. THORNTON again came alongside at 1304 to furnish power for submersible pumps and remained until the following morning. During the night of the eighteenth, CHINCOTEAGUE remained dead in the water with THORNTON alongside. JENKINS (DD447) and TREVER (DMS16) acted as anti-submarine screen. Pumping and bucket brigades continued without stop.

24.   Heavy seas forced THORNTON to cast off on the morning of 19 July. The tug SONOMA (AT12) came alongside at 1113 with additional pumping equipment and took CHINCOTEAGUE in tow, arriving at Espiritu Santo at 0825 on 21 July. After temporary repairs to make the hull watertight were accomplished, CHINCOTEAGUE was towed to Navy Yard, Mare Island, arriving 4 September 1943. All battle damage was repaired and many authorized alterations completed. The vessel is now back in service.

Sailing Home

What is it the billowing waves impart,
and repeat and repeat with each dash
What is the pounding in my heart?
I'm sailing home at last.

The salt spray stings on the naked cheek
and the wind sings in the mast,
but it only sings because it knows,
I'm sailing home, at last.

Was it centuries since we sailed away
Out of the harbor there,
or was it only yesterday
I dont know, nor care.

For gone are the lonely nights and the days
mid tropical isles alone
and gone is the hunger countenanced there.
At last I'm sailing home.

And tho the sailor sails the seas
and in distant places roam
There is no "call" thats quite so sweet
as the call "I'm Sailing Home"

By Sherman Walgren May 1942
aboard U.S.S. NORTHAMPTON

USS CHINCOTEAGUE AVP 24
April 12, 1943 - December 21, 1946

12 April 1943	PSNY Bremerton, Wash. U.S.S. Chincoteague commissioned into the fleet
April 1943	Seattle, Wash.
May 1943	San Francisco, Calif.
June 1943	San Diego, Calif.
June 1943	Pearl Harbor, Oahu, Territory of Hawaii
July 1943	Espirito Santo, New Hebrides Islands[A]
July 1943	Saboe Bay, Vanikoro, Santa Cruz Islands
16 July 1943	Air Attack, Saboe Bay (Heavy Damage)
21 July 1943	Espirito Santo, New Hebrides Islands[A] (Emergency Repairs)
August 1943	MINY, Vallejo, Calif. (For Overhaul)
January 1944	San Diego, Calif.
January 1944	Pearl Harbor, Oahu, Territory of Hawaii
February 1944	Kwajalein Atoll, Marshall Islands
February 1944	Enawetak Atoll, Marshall Islands
March 1944	Majuro Atoll, Marshall Islands
March 1944	Tarawa Atoll, Gilbert Islands [B]
April 1944	Funafuti Atoll, Tuvalu Islands
April 1944	Espirito Santo, New Hebrides Islands[A]
May 1944	Guadalcanal Island, Solomon Islands
May 1944	Tulagi Island, Solomon Islands
May 1944	Green Island, Bismark Archipelago
June 1944	Treasury Islands, Shortland Islands, Bismark Archipelago

June 1944	Tulagi Island, Solomon Islands
June 1944	Espirito Santo, New Hebrides Islands[A]
June 1944	Munda, New Georgia Island, New Georgia Islands
July 1944	Efate Island, New Hebrides Islands[A]
July 1944	Malakula Island, New Hebrides Islands[A]
July 1944	Efate Island, New Hebrides Islands[A]
July 1944	Espirito Santo, New Hebrides Islands[A]
July 1944	Malakula Island, New Hebrides Islands[A]
August 1944	Halavo, Florida Island, New Hebrides Islands[A]
August 1944	Malakula Island, New Hebrides Islands[A]
August 1944	Auckland, New Zealand
August 1944	Malakula Island, New Hebrides Islands[A]
August 1944	Guadalcanal Island, Solomon Islands
August 1944	Halavo, Florida Island, New Hebrides Islands[A]
September 1944	Malakula Island, New Hebrides Islands[A]
September 1944	Esperito Santo, New Hebrides Islands[A]
September 1944	Enawetak Atoll, Marshall Islands
September 1944	Saipan, Mariana Islands
September 1944	Enawetak Atoll, Marshall Islands
October 1944	Pearl Harbor, Oahu, Territory of Hawaii
October 1944	Maui Island, Oahu, Territory of Hawaii
October 1944	Pearl Harbor, Oahu, Territory of Hawaii
October 1944	Maui Island, Oahu, Territory of Hawaii
October 1944	Pearl Harbor, Oahu, Territory of Hawaii
October 1944	Maui Island, Oahu, Territory of Hawaii
October 1944	Pearl Harbor, Oahu, Territory of Hawaii
November 1944	Enawetak, Marshall Islands

December 1944	Eulithi Atoll, Yap Islands [C]
6 December 1944	Kossol Roads, Palau Islands
December 1944	Pelelu Atoll, Palau Islands
December 1944	Kossol Roads, Palau Islands
January 1945	Pelelu Atoll, Palau Islands
February 1945	Kossol Roads, Palau Islands
February 1945	Saipan, Mariana Islands
13 February 1945	Guam, Mariana Islands
20 February 1945	Iwo Jima, Volcano Islands
March 1945	Saipan, Mariana Islands
March 1945	Guam, Mariana Islands
March 1945	Eulithi Atoll, Yap Islands
June 1945	Pearl Harbor, Oahu, Territory of Hawaii
June 1945	Maui Island, Territory of Hawaii
June 1945	Pearl Harbor, Oahu, Territory of Hawaii
June 1945	Nob Terminal Island, San Pedro, Calif. (Overhaul)
3 October 1945 – 16 March 1946	Occupation Duty at Okinawa and Tsingtao, China. Then back home to: San Diego, California New Orleans, Louisiana Beaumont, Texas
2 December 1946	USS Chincoteague (AVP 24) was decommissioned from the fleet and placed in reserve.

(A) Vanuatu Islands — New Hebrides Islands
(B) Kiribati Islands — Gilbert Islands
(C) Yap Islands — Part of the Federated States of Micronesia